The One Minute Father

Other Books by Spencer Johnson, M.D.

YES OR NO
The Guide to Better Decisions

THE PRECIOUS PRESENT
The Gift That Makes a Person Happy Forever

THE ONE MINUTE MANAGER
Increase Productivity, Profits, and Your Own Prosperity
(co-authored with Kenneth Blanchard, Ph.D.)

THE ONE MINUTE $ALES PERSON
The Quickest Way to More Sales with Less Stress
(co-authored with Larry Wilson)

THE ONE MINUTE MOTHER
The Quickest Way for You
to Help Your Children Learn to Like Themselves
and Want to Behave Themselves

THE ONE MINUTE TEACHER
How to Teach Others to Teach Themselves
(co-authored with Constance Johnson, M.Ed.)

ONE MINUTE FOR MYSELF
How to Manage Your Most Valuable Asset

THE VALUETALES SERIES FOR CHILDREN:

The Value of Believing in Yourself: The Story of Louis Pasteur

The Value of Patience: The Story of the Wright Brothers

The Value of Kindness: The Story of Elizabeth Fry

The Value of Humor: The Story of Will Rogers

The Value of Courage: The Story of Jackie Robinson

The Value of Curiosity: The Story of Christopher Columbus

The Value of Imagination: The Story of Charles Dickens

The Value of Saving: The Story of Ben Franklin

The Value of Sharing: The Story of the Mayo Brothers

The Value of Honesty: The Story of Confucius

The Value of Understanding: The Story of Margaret Mead

The Value of Fantasy: The Story of Hans Christian Andersen

The Value of Dedication: The Story of Albert Schweitzer

The One Minute Father

The Quickest Way for You to
Help Your Children
Learn to Like Themselves
and Want to Behave Themselves

Spencer Johnson, M.D.

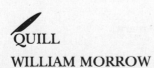

QUILL

WILLIAM MORROW

New York

It is the policy of William Morrow and Company, Inc., and its
imprints and affiliates, recognizing the importance of preserving
what has been written, to print the books we publish on acid-free
paper, and we exert our best efforts to that end.

Library of Congress Catalog Card Number: 83-62159

ISBN: 0-688-14405-5

Printed in the United States of America

4 5 6 7 8 9 10

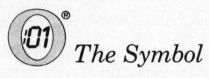 *The Symbol*

The One Minute Father's symbol—a one-minute readout from the face of a modern digital watch—is intended to remind each of us to take a minute out of our day, every now and then, and look into the faces of our children.

Dedicated to
Emerson, Christian and Austin

Contents

A Letter to Fathers:

You certainly know from your own experience that being a good father takes more than a minute.

However, there are ways you can communicate with your children—in only a minute—that will help them quickly learn how to like themselves and want to behave themselves.

The techniques are so simple, it may be difficult for you to believe that they will work.

Nonetheless, you may want to do as other parents have successfully done—suspend passing judgment on the three communication methods you're going to read about until you have actually used them in your own home for one month.

Then judge for yourself. See how your children's behavior improves. And ask your children how good they feel about themselves.

I'm sure you will find what I and other practical parents have found with our children: From both the children's and the parent's point of view, it works!

Spencer Johnson

SPENCER JOHNSON, M.D.

The One Minute Father

ONE day a successful man saw that he was lost—and had been for some time. He began at once to look for an answer to a problem he had never even realized he had.

It began soon after the sudden death of his wife. He was left alone with his five children.

He and his wife had both tried as well as they knew how to raise their children with love and discipline. They did, basically, what they had seen their parents do.

The man never realized, however, how difficult parenting was on a day-in and day-out basis—and how much his wife had assumed that responsibility.

He was beginning to understand what she had been trying to tell him.

Now the more time The Father spent around his children, the more he realized how unaware he had been. He remembered how often his wife had said that she was frustrated because she felt the situation with the children was getting worse. But he never wanted to acknowledge the problem.

The man now saw how challenging her task had been. He knew now that it would have been better if they had mutually supported each other in the raising of their children.

The man then began to look at his children's behavior—undisguised by their mother's peacekeeping and nurturing ways.

He wondered how often she had simply been trying to protect him from his children's misbehavior. Or was it they who had been protected from him?

The more he saw for himself, the more he realized how unruly his children were; how unappreciative they seemed of all that he and their mother had done. And what was that look in their eyes—their own confusion?

He knew he had started his family later in life than most men—he'd been so busy. But was he that much out of touch with the younger generation?

Were all children this way? How and when did *his* children get this way?

As time went by, The Father began to see the beginnings of serious problems in his family—the kind he had only read about—and always, of course, in other families.

For the first time, he began to be disturbed by the news reports on television and in the newspapers. He didn't want to think about the things he knew were happening elsewhere: the increasing incidence of juvenile drug use, vandalism, illegitimacy, delinquency—even violent crime and suicide. It was too disquieting.

He tried to block it all out of his mind. But when he saw his own children staying away from home a little longer, a little more often, he thought about the increasing problem of juvenile runaways.

He allowed himself for a moment to realize that families everywhere were experiencing the personal pain behind the impersonal statistics.

The man loved his children. He decided to do something about it.

But what? What would he do first?

The once unaware man now looked at his family with new eyes. Then he saw what he hoped was the answer.

"I have not held my children accountable," he thought. "They get away with a great deal. And that is not good for them—or for me.

"What my children need is more *discipline!*" he decided. And the man was right. His children did need more discipline. And so he began to discipline them more—the best way he knew how.

At first the man did more of what his parents had done. Whenever his children misbehaved, he either grounded them, threatened them, sent them to their rooms, removed their privileges, or spanked them.

But he did not get the results he wanted.

So he disciplined them even more—doing more of what he had already done. He was exhausting himself, but his children's behavior improved— temporarily.

Their attitudes, however, did not. They grew more obedient on the outside but more resentful on the inside.

The man could feel the tension in his home. He was becoming frustrated. It seemed as if the harder he tried, the worse the situation became.

He knew that he did not know what to do. However, The Father had been in this situation in other areas of his life and he had always found a successful answer. So he did what had worked for him so many times before.

He looked for someone who knew.

THE man introduced himself to the physician who had just poured him a cup of coffee. He explained, "I don't know why I can't run my family as well as I run some of the other aspects of my life."

The physician, who specialized in family behavior, said, "I know what you must be feeling."

Then he quietly asked, "Why do you think you have to 'run' your family?"

The man paused and listened. He hadn't thought of that before. He assumed that it was his responsibility. As he listened—especially to himself—he began to learn.

"Which do you think would be easier on you," the man was asked, "to run your children's lives or to have them successfully run their own lives?"

"Now that you ask, I guess I'd like them to be able to decide wisely what is right for them. I want what all parents want. I'd like my children to be happy and to grow up to become the kind of people they would like to be."

"What is your biggest problem now?" the physician continued.

"Discipline!" he answered. "I can't even get them to behave for me, let alone be happy."

"Behave for *you*?" the physician asked.

"OK, OK," the man said with his hands raised in mock surrender, "for *themselves*."

The physician laughed—he liked this man. "I'm also a father," he said, "and I face the same challenges. I have been fortunate, however, to discover a method of discipline that takes very little time and yet works wonders for the family."

The man looked both hopeful and embarrassed.

"I'm afraid I've taken very little time so far with my children," the man admitted. "I'm not so concerned about how much time it takes me as I am about how much it will help my children and me. I want things to be better for my family."

"You want the best for your children and that is admirable. But would you mind if you could get very good results in very little time?"

The man laughed and said, "I'd love it! How soon can I learn it?"

"You can *learn* about the discipline method very quickly, although it may take you a few weeks of using it before you learn to do it well yourself.

"In fact, when you first use this discipline method, it will be different, and so you may not feel as if you are being 'yourself.'"

"Like when I first learned a better golf swing," the man suggested. "I felt that the new way was not 'me.' But then after a while it felt more natural. And I was very glad that I had changed."

"If you understand that and are willing to change the way you discipline, I have good news.

"You can learn to discipline your children so they will *want* to behave themselves.

"And the best part is that you and your children will come to respect and to enjoy each other more."

"It sounds terrific! Where do we start?"

"Let's begin by looking at what good discipline is. The word *discipline* itself comes to us from the Latin word *disciplina* which means 'teaching.'

"Our job as fathers is simply to teach our children the advantages of *self*-discipline."

"It sounds to me," the father noted, "as if the kind of discipline you're talking about would make me more of a teacher and less of a punisher.

"How would I go about it?"

"The method I use is deceptively simple and easy to learn. It takes only a minute to do, so I call it 'The One Minute Reprimand.'"

"The what?" the astonished man asked. He believed somehow that good discipline would be complicated. "With all due respect, Doctor, it sounds so simple that I'm afraid that it probably wouldn't work with my children."

"I can understand your skepticism. All my professional training leads me to question anything that might be simplistic.

"However, while I don't like to make promises, I can assure you that if you use the method *properly*, you will get the results you're looking for."

The man decided to put his doubts aside and listen. If it was true, it was exactly the kind of discipline he had been trying to find.

"What do I do first?" the man asked.

"Let's begin to understand what you are going to do," the physician suggested, "by knowing what you want to achieve as a result of the reprimand."

"Before you *do* anything, remind yourself that:

*

*When I Discipline
My Children,
I Want Them To Feel
Bad About
Their Misbehavior*

*But Good
About Themselves*

*

The man thought for a moment. "That's very interesting," he said. "I never thought about the difference between how children feel about their *behavior* and how they see *themselves*. I thought they were pretty much the same thing."

"I'm glad you said that. That is why most reprimands do not work very well. Children are like the rest of us. Whenever someone attacks our behavior, as though it were the same as our worth, we get defensive. And then what do we do?"

"We defend our behavior," The Father said.

"Yes, of course," the physician responded. "Even if we know we were wrong."

"That's exactly what happens with my children," The Father admitted. "Frankly, I'm ready to learn a better way. Where do I start?"

The physician was very specific. "Deal with each child as an individual and in private.

"Even though you may be very angry with their behavior, it is important for you to be aware of your real feelings. If you love your children, you feel two things: real anger and real love. So verbalize *both*!

"Just remember, before you begin to reprimand them, what your key to success is: Your children's *behavior* is *not* OK, but they *are* OK.

"Then look your child straight in the eye.

"Say very clearly what your child has *done*. Be as specific as you can. It takes only a few seconds.

"'You have come home very late! You did not tell me where you were going! This is the second time this week!'

"Next, tell your child in no uncertain terms how you *feel* about what he or she has done.

"'I AM ANGRY. I AM VERY ANGRY!'

"If you are angry, express anger *angrily*.

"If you are annoyed, express it with annoyance.

"'I AM ANNOYED. I AM VERY ANNOYED.'

"If you are sad, be sad. In short, express whatever you really feel—honestly and emotionally.

"The most important part of the first half of the One Minute Reprimand is that you want your children to *feel* what you are feeling.

"They will know that you are upset just from the fact that they are receiving a reprimand. You want your children to do more than just know you are upset; you want them to *feel* it.

"It will not hurt your children for you to 'tell it like it is.' It will simply help them learn.

"Just remember your children are not your punching bags," the doctor cautioned. "Do not go on and on about it. It doesn't take long to let someone know how you feel.

"In as little as half a minute you can let them know in no uncertain terms.

"Then pause . . .

"You want your child to *feel* your feelings. So just let the unpleasant silence hang in the air.

"During these uncomfortable few seconds, the children won't like it—or *you* at that moment.

"The typical feelings of resentment will begin to occur. No one likes to be reprimanded. But that is exactly what you want from the first part of the Reprimand. You want it to be unpleasant."

After the man thought for a while about what he had just heard, he spoke quietly, "I must say, the first half of the One Minute Reprimand is brief but I could almost feel the discomfort myself as I listened to you express your anger. And I wasn't even the one being reprimanded."

"Believe me," the physician said, "although it doesn't last long, receiving a One Minute Reprimand is not a pleasant experience."

The Father nodded and continued to think.

Then he asked, "So how do I solve the problem of my children resenting me for it and becoming defensive and unpleasant themselves?"

"By doing the last half of the Reprimand," the physician said. "It's the key to success.

"If you do not do it, the Reprimand will not be effective. If you *do* do the last half of the One Minute Reprimand, it will work. Your children will choose to dramatically improve their own behavior.

"I must remind you, however," the physician cautioned, "that while it is simple to do once you have learned to do it, it is not easy at first—especially if you are not used to doing it. It will require a significant change in your behavior."

"I understand," The Father said. "But I really do want to find a better way. What do I do next?"

"In the first half of the minute, you have emotionally told your child the truth—you are angry/frustrated/sad with his *behavior*!

"Now take a deep breath and calm down. When you are ready, look at and *touch* your child in a way that lets him know you are on his side.

"Then for the next half minute or so, quietly tell your child the *rest* of the truth. It is what he wants and needs to hear most from you right now: that he is a good person and that you love him.

"I know it may be difficult to do the second half of the Reprimand but it is by far the more important part. Just keep it honest and brief:

"'Your behavior tonight was not good. But *you* are good! That's why I'm so upset. You're better than that kind of behavior. I know you are a good person. And I love you—a lot!'

"Then give your child a quick hug to let him know that the Reprimand is over. When it's over, it's *over*. You don't mention it again."

The Father reflected on what he had heard. It was amazing to think that something so simple could work so well. "It's literally hard to believe."

"I know," the physician acknowledged. "But the more you believe it and do it, no matter how hard your children resist, the faster you and your children will get the marvelous results you are all looking for—just as other families have.

"Speaking of families," the physician said, "a few of them taught me something very important."

"What is that?" The Father asked.

"When I first developed this method, I thought of it as a discipline method. When you begin, it will be just that. And it will be very effective."

"And later on?" The Father inquired.

"After you have used it for a while with your children, you will see that, although it acts as discipline, it is really *communication* at its best.

"And that is when you will begin to see another use for this method. It will become more than just a way for *you* to communicate with your children."

"You mean," the man interjected, "that it will become a way for them to communicate with me?"

"Yes. Your children undoubtedly have some pent-up feelings and frustrations of their own."

"Are you saying," the man asked, "that I should encourage them to be just as honest with me?"

"Yes, when you are ready," the man was told.

"Use the Reprimand for a while yourself and see how quickly it clears the air and improves things at home. Then when you have enough experience and confidence with using it, you might suggest that your children do the same with you.

"Families who are using the method have found from their own experiences that it works better when the communications flow freely and equally.

"When your children have seen you express your feelings without attacking the other person, they will be more apt to tell you honestly how they feel without being inconsiderate or rude to you."

The Father said, "Fine. I'm going to try it!"

Then he wrote down a summary as though he were already using what he had just learned.

The One Minute Reprimand works well when:

1. I tell my children beforehand that I am going to reprimand them when their behavior is unacceptable to me. And I encourage them to be just as honest with me.

The First Half of the Reprimand

2. I reprimand my children as *soon* as possible.
3. I tell them *specifically* what they did.
4. I tell my children, in no uncertain terms, just how I *feel* about what they have done.
5. I am silent for a few very long, unpleasant seconds—to let them *feel* what I feel.

The Second Half of the Reprimand

6. Then I calm down and *touch* my children in a way that lets them know that I am on their side.
7. I remind my children that while their recent behavior was not good, I think *they* are good.
8. I tell my children, "I love you!" And I hug them. When the Reprimand is over—it's *over*. I don't mention it again.
9. Later in the day, I listen to whatever the children want to tell me.
10. I realize that while it may take me only a minute to reprimand my children with love, the benefits may last them for a *lifetime*.

The man stood up, shook hands, and thanked the physician. He was told that he could telephone anytime with the questions that were bound to arise as he began to use the One Minute Reprimand in his own home.

As he walked back to his car, the man thought, "This sounds simple enough. But I know it's going to require a change in *my* behavior. And that's not going to be quite so simple!

"I wonder if I can tell my kids how I feel? I haven't always found that easy to do.

"And I wonder if I can calm down after telling them in no uncertain terms how I feel about their behavior. I hope I can remember to remind them that they are good. And to tell them that I love them." But the man knew that as a child, he would have liked to have heard such words.

As he thought about changing the way he disciplined his children, he was uncomfortable.

Then he decided that gaining a better family was worth the temporary discomfort of his trying something new. He knew he was going to try.

As he returned to his car, he scanned his mind for a "hook"—a thought he could hang onto as he began to use this new method of discipline.

Then he made an important note. It was a single sentence which he wrote in positive language.

He hadn't realized it yet, but this invaluable first lesson would eventually lead him to discover for himself the more complete answer he was looking for.

He reread the sentence several times:

*

The More Children
Like Themselves

The More They
Like To Behave Themselves

*

AFTER the man arrived home, he met with his five children. He knew it would be an uncomfortable gathering but he hoped it would be a useful one.

"I would like to be a better father," he admitted. "And frankly," he added with a smile, "I wouldn't mind if you kids acted a little better yourselves.

"I've been working so hard to be a success elsewhere," he said, "I'm afraid I've neglected some of the most important parts of my life—you!"

Then The Father told his children what he had learned about the One Minute Reprimand. They asked questions which he answered honestly.

The Father told his children that he would have preferred such discipline when he was a child himself—but he was never given a choice.

Then he gave each child just such a choice.

When they misbehaved, they could get more of the same kind of punishment they now received, or they could get a One Minute Reprimand.

Neither seemed appealling. No one spoke.

"Giving my children a One Minute Reprimand when they misbehave," he thought, "is something I am going to do *for* my children, not something I am going to do *to* them."

The Father knew from his work that when people participate in a decision that affects them, they are more apt to want it to succeed.

Then The Father said, "Think of it as a bet where you can either win or break even. If it helps us enjoy a happier home, we win. If not, we break even—things will stay pretty much the same."

The older boy, who had grown into a resentful teenager, said, "Who cares? It's not going to make any difference anyway."

The Father replied, "Fine. I'll just go right on disciplining you the way I always have if that is what you really want." Then he turned and asked, "What about the rest of you?"

The other children had grown tired of their older brother's attitude. "It sounds fair to me," the middle daughter said. "Me too," the older girl decided. The nine-year-old boy asked quietly, "Can I wait and see how this all turns out?"

The Father laughed. "OK," he said with a false growl, "I'll just go right on spanking you."

"Oh," the youngster said. "Now that I think of it, I think a Reprimand would be better."

Then The Father did a very wise thing. He honestly admitted, "To tell you the truth, I don't know if I can do it—or do it very *well*. I'm not good at expressing my feelings. I've never seen my own dad do it. I just don't know if I can change!"

The older boy said, "You could at least *try*!"

The man didn't know if his older son's comment was resentful or hopeful. But he saw it as ironic that the child who had said it wouldn't make any difference had asked him to try.

The children came to appreciate their father more because he told them the truth up front about the Reprimand, gave them each a choice and frankly admitted that he wouldn't always do it just right.

The Father then began to use the One Minute Reprimand with four of his five children.

As soon as The Father began to use the Reprimand he met resistance from every one of his children.

All of them, in their own way, tried everything they could think of to get their father to stop using the painful method of discipline.

They wouldn't look at their father while he was speaking to them. They stared out the window and acted bored. They looked up at the ceiling with annoyance—anything to avoid their father's eyes.

They laughed nervously and made light of what they were being told.

The toddler covered her ears with her tiny hands and pressed her lips tightly together, shutting out all the world around her.

The younger boy's favorite trick was to look at his wrist to read the imaginary watch he didn't own. He was timing his father.

He knew he was receiving a One Minute Reprimand. And he wanted his father to know that he knew what was going on.

They tried to walk away, of course, and just not listen to any more.

But The Father persisted.

No matter what the children did to dilute the effect of the Reprimand, The Father continued. He expressed himself in no uncertain terms.

Before long the children began to feel his anger or frustration or sadness or whatever else he was really feeling about their behavior. They knew it was not acceptable to him. And they didn't like the feeling.

But what hurt most was the moment when he calmed down, touched them in a caring way, and told them they were better than such behavior.

And then he reminded them of how much he loved them. It was what they really wanted to hear. But you would never know it from their behavior—at least not at first.

In the beginning, the children talked back in the middle of a Reprimand. They had explanations for what they had done and they wanted to tell him about each one. They tried vigorously to defend their behavior—even if they knew they were wrong.

But every time they did so, an already annoyed father reminded them in a loud voice, "This is not a discussion! I am telling you just exactly how I feel! And if you want this to go on longer, I will continue to tell you!"

The children soon learned that no matter what they did, their father would let them know in no uncertain terms just exactly how he felt about their unacceptable behavior.

And later he did something that made a very big difference to his family. He encouraged his children to come back at other times and to tell him anything they wanted him to hear.

Most of the time, after the children had thought about what their father had said, they knew he had been fair, and they didn't need to talk again.

However, when they did come back to speak to him, he *listened* intensely. He wanted his children to listen to him when he spoke. And he knew:

*

The Best Way
To Get My Children
To Listen

Is
To Listen

*

After only a few weeks the man noticed a big improvement in the behavior of most of his children. It didn't happen all at once, of course. And he did not achieve success painlessly.

Although he had been told that the Reprimand would work, still The Father was surprised to see how dramatic the improvements were.

Curious, he asked his younger son one day what he thought of the One Minute Reprimand as discipline.

"I don't like it," the boy said. "It hurts too much and it lasts too long."

When his surprised father heard this, he asked, "It doesn't hurt as much as a spanking, does it?"

"The Reprimand hurts a lot more, Dad. I don't like the way I feel lousy about what I did. And my feeling lasts a lot longer than a spanking. I keep thinking about what you said—that *I'm* better."

The Father knew he had found an answer.

He soon saw more than his children's obviously improved behavior. He saw and felt the better relationship he was developing with them.

They apparently did feel bad about their misbehavior but good about themselves. And what pleased him most, they felt closer to *him*.

The children were learning three things: They were not going to get away with unacceptable behavior, they were good, and they were loved.

The Father had always loved his children, of course. But as soon as he had begun to use the One Minute Reprimand, he and his children began to experience a much happier homelife.

He thought about the difference:

*

*There Is
A Big Difference
Between
Being Loved
And Feeling Loved*

*

The Father's children began to feel loved because their father *expressed* his love for them.

As he had expected, he had found it difficult in the beginning to express both angry and loving feelings so close to each other. When he got angry, he sometimes forgot to remind his children that *they* were good and that he loved them.

However, simply by doing it many times, over and over, he got better and better at it.

He expressed his feelings about his children's poor behavior, *emotionally* and in no uncertain terms, and then he quietly told them how much he loved them—even when their behavior was unacceptable.

After he had developed his own confidence, he began to encourage his children to be just as honest with him about *their* feelings.

One by one, they came to him in private and expressed how they really felt. They did indeed have some anger and frustrations of their own. And they told their father in no uncertain terms!

And then they told their dad how much they really loved him. And they gave him great hugs. Sometimes they held on so long that it embarrassed him. But he loved it.

Finally the man's resentful teenage son came to him. He was in the worst trouble he had ever been in and seemingly didn't know where else to turn.

The boy had seen the good things that were happening between his father and his brother and sisters and he somehow wanted to be a part of it.

He decided to take a chance. He told his father the truth.

After he had told his father the obviously bad thing he had done, the teenager didn't know what else to say. But it was clear that he was asking for help.

The Father had a lot of love as well as a good deal of built-up frustration and anger toward his belligerent son. For some reason, it was more difficult for him to tell his firstborn how he felt. But he knew it was what the boy needed and what he was asking for.

The Reprimand was long overdue.

The Father looked him straight in the eye and said, "You have destroyed someone else's property—literally destroyed it! You know better than that!

"Your behavior has been unacceptable! And I'm tired of it! I am frustrated. And I am angry!"

The Father's face was turning red and the veins were standing out on his neck.

He was just beginning to get out the anger that had been there for years. But he was brief. He knew that he would have other opportunities to express his anger—although just as briefly.

He looked his son in the eyes and quickly repeated for the second time, "I am angry!!!"

During the brief but deadly silence that followed, the boy felt his father's anger.

He did not like what he was experiencing.

At that moment, the youngster disliked his father. And he resented the way he was being spoken to. He began to think of all the reasons he had had for doing what he had done.

He was just about to talk back when . . .

The Father took a deep breath, and then gently placed his hand on his son's shoulder.

He said quietly, "Son, you not only *know* better. You *are* better! You're going to have to replace what you have destroyed. But you can do it. You're a good person. You know that and I know that. You are a good and worthwhile person, son!"

The Father paused. Then he said, "And I love you." The man gave his son a big hug.

The boy didn't know what to do. He started to hug his father but then pulled away and walked off.

Later the teenager readily agreed to replace what he had destroyed. He returned a few days after that to talk with his father. But he still wasn't comfortable. "Thanks, Dad" was all he said.

The Father heard a great deal more.

Soon the man found that he was using the One Minute Reprimand as his *only* method of discipline with all his children.

Within a few short months, he was getting very good results. Every child seemed to want to behave better. Even the older boy, whom he had to reprimand more frequently than the others, had improved—both his behavior and attitude.

The children were really beginning to feel good about *themselves*.

The family was beginning to enjoy being a family. The Father wished he had learned about the Reprimand when his wife was alive. They would all have enjoyed life more.

Things were going very well, in fact, until the "supermarket incident."

THE man had taken his children shopping for a few groceries. His youngest daughter was sitting in the folded-out toddler's chair in the shopping cart. Without warning, she began to whine and beg for Daddy to place all "the goodies" in the cart for her. She then began to pull things off the nearby shelves and send them plummeting into the cart. Her whining grew worse.

The Father had always thought that the sound of a whining child reminded him, at best, of someone dragging fingernails across a blackboard. He had made that known to his children.

When The Father gave his little daughter a look that said "You've got it coming now, kiddo!," the little girl smiled. Then she grinned a happy look and said joyfully, "Rep-me-man, Daddy? Rep-me-man?"

The Father thought, "This isn't working out. She's supposed to want to avoid a Reprimand, not look forward to it."

The disquieted Father wheeled his youngster outside where, in private, he gave her a very brief but spirited Reprimand for her unacceptable behavior.

The little girl soon seemed to feel better. She relaxed and gave her dad a big hug. She was very good for the rest of the day.

But The Father was confused. "What is it I'm doing wrong?" he asked himself.

The Father drove home from the supermarket, his car full of groceries and children. The youngsters vied for his attention.

However, he was deep in thought.

"There just has to be a better way," he reflected. "I don't want to do nothing but reprimand my children. It is tiring. And I can certainly think of better ways to spend time with them."

The Father had to admit, however, that he was a lot *less* tired since he had begun to use only this faster and more effective discipline method.

"Still," he thought, "there has to be a better way. There is more to good parenting than good discipline.

"I want my children to do more than act well-behaved. I want them to think of themselves as individual winners—each in his or her own way. But how do I do that?"

The Father continued to drive and think.

He looked at the car in front of him. The bumper sticker caught his eye.

It read:

*

Have You
Hugged
Your Child
Today?

*

To The Father's surprise, his immediate reaction was "No! That is . . . not unless . . . it's at the end . . . of a One Minute Reprimand."

The Father then knew what his children had been trying to tell him. He realized why his teenage son had gotten into the worst trouble he'd been in lately. And he knew why his little girl had misbehaved in the supermarket.

"It was the best way," The Father now saw, "to get my undivided attention for at least one full minute! It was the one sure way to get a hug from me and to hear me say 'I love you'!"

In that moment, The Father also realized that he had done nothing when the children behaved.

Nothing! Absolutely nothing.

One of the children began to act up in the car and it attracted his attention.

He looked at his children. Then he laughed.

"What's so funny, Daddy?" the oldest girl asked.

"I just thought of a joke," he said, "one I played on myself." He promised, "I'll tell you later, honey." And he knew he would.

Then he turned back to his thoughts. At first, the man was defensive with himself. "Why *should* I have done anything when my children weren't misbehaving," he thought. "They were just doing what they were supposed to be doing. My parents didn't do anything when *I* behaved."

Then the man indeed found a better way.

He decided that was the last day his children would have to *mis*behave in order to get his full attention.

The Father was glad it was the beginning of a weekend. It would give him time to do something different with his children.

After they all got home, the man watched his two older daughters at play in the yard. Then he saw what he was looking for.

When he spoke, he startled his two children. "Young ladies, come in here right now!"

The girls looked at each other as if to say "What did *we* do?" They couldn't imagine what they had done wrong.

They came in to their father—reluctantly.

The children had felt closer to their father over the last few months. And they had grown to love him more. But they also still feared him.

"I saw what you just did," The Father said. He looked at them, touched each of them and said, "I saw you two share your things with each other."

The two girls smiled at one another.

Then The Father smiled too and said, "I want you to know how happy I am. I feel very good knowing what generous young ladies I have for children. I'm really glad you two live in our house!"

The Father briefly hugged each of his daughters and said, "I love you!"

The children just stood there looking at their father. When he didn't say anything, they slowly turned and walked away. They weren't sure what to make of it. But they smiled. And they felt good.

His children didn't know it yet, but the man had made a decision as he was driving. He was going to start catching his children doing something *right!*

And when he did, he was going to give them something he had just invented himself—"A One Minute Praising." It would be a gift he would give to his children—frequently.

The Father smiled as he saw his young daughters' reaction. He was pleased that he had acted on his decision so soon. He thought, "If they're amazed, I can hardly wait to see my older boy's reaction."

The Father had to admit that while he still did not like some of his older boy's attitudes, he knew that they were due, in part, to the fact that the boy had been ignored for so long.

The man was not going to apologize constantly for his past behavior. And he was not going to accept the responsibility for the boy's attitude either.

In fact, The Father had given the boy more than one effective Reprimand for his bad attitude.

However, The Father knew that his son was basically good.

He had decided that if he waited until his son did something perfectly right, he might have to wait a *very* long time.

So he decided he would catch his teenager doing something *approximately* right.

While he waited for an appropriate opportunity with his son, he thought about what he was doing for his children.

*

*I Help My Children
Realize They Are
Already Winners.*

*I Catch Them Doing
Something <u>Right</u>!*

*

Before long, the man's teenage son came into the room. The Father and son hadn't talked much, except occasionally after a Reprimand.

"Can I borrow the car?" the boy asked in a surly tone. The words *Dad* and *please* were still not part of the resentful teenager's vocabulary.

"Sure," the boy heard to his amazement.

The Father knew that what he was about to do next would be neither believed nor trusted by his son—at least not at first. But the man decided that from now on he would simply tell the boy the truth.

"The simple truth will eventually win out," The Father reminded himself. "The truth is the only thing he'll trust."

Then The Father went over and briefly touched his older boy's shoulder. "Thanks for asking, son.

"I appreciate it when you ask permission. Some kids just *take* the car. And that leads to problems. You *ask*." Then he added, "You're a *good man!*"

At first the boy didn't know what to say. He mumbled, "Thanks."

The Father smiled, touched his son briefly on the forearm, and said, "I love you."

The man returned to his chair. It had taken less than a minute.

As the boy left the room, he looked back over his shoulder at his father.

By the end of the second day of unannounced One Minute Praisings, all five children had noticed the change in their father.

And they all wondered what was happening.

After dinner, The Father gathered all his children together and said, "I imagine you're wondering what's going on."

"You'd better believe it!" the younger son said.

"Well, let me tell you," The Father offered.

The man turned to his eldest daughter and said, "Remember, honey, when we were riding in the car and you asked me what I was laughing about? And I said it was a joke—one I'd played on myself?"

"Yes," she said, delighted that her father had remembered. "And you promised you'd tell me."

"Well, as I was driving along I was admitting to myself that I really don't pay that much attention to you children when you behave well. I pay attention to you when you *mis*behave."

Then The Father smiled. "And just as I was thinking that, one of you started to misbehave."

The children grinned. One of them laughed.

"Well, I started to laugh too," The Father said, "because it was a great example of what happens in our family. I wasn't paying attention to any of you. So what did one of you do?"

"I started arguing with my little brother," one of the girls admitted.

"Well now, how would you like it if sometimes I did notice you when you are doing well?"

"Sure. That would be great," the daughter said.

Under his breath, just loud enough for everyone to hear, the teenage boy said, "It's *about time*."

The Father gave his son a look that showed he was annoyed by the boy's comment.

"Sorry," the boy said slowly. "I'm sorry."

The whole family was amazed. It was the first decent thing the boy had said to his father for some time. The boy was beginning to change.

The Father smiled and nodded his thanks.

Then he said, "The truth is, son, you are right. It *is* about time.

"And I think it's also about time," The Father noted, "that you and I started to treat one another the way we would each like to be treated.

"It is tough enough out there in the real world without beating each other up at home.

"We would all do better if we started catching each other at home doing something *right*!"

No one spoke but everyone agreed.

"It makes life easier," The Father said, "when we know how we are really doing. So I am going to try to help you by letting you know when you are doing well and when you are doing poorly.

"When you're doing something I don't like, I'll let you know," The Father said.

"Tell us about it!" the little boy said.

Everyone laughed, including The Father. "I have been good about *that* lately, haven't I?"

"Yes," the eldest daughter said. "You have. And to tell you the truth, Dad, it's helped."

She went over and gave her dad a hug and said, "I love you." No one said anything. But everyone felt the love in the room.

Finally The Father spoke. "Thanks, honey. That felt good. You know *I* could also use some Praisings. Parents are people too!"

The children had never thought of that.

Then the younger boy grinned and said, "I really like your idea, Dad, about giving us One Minute Praisings." He thought for a moment.

Then the youngster went over to his dad, put his little hand up on his father's big shoulder, looked him straight in the eye, and said, "You talk to us more now, Dad. In fact, you treat us like we're real people. And I want you to know how I feel about that. I feel *real good!*"

The children all laughed—even the older boy. They all knew a One Minute Praising when they heard one. And they all enjoyed it.

Then the little boy quietly said, "I love you too, Dad." He hugged his father very tightly.

The man started to choke up. But he hid it from his children. When he recovered, he said with a laugh, "Thanks, son. I needed that."

The man hadn't learned yet to let his children see his deepest feelings. And he also knew that he wasn't always as good at talking about his feelings with his children as he would like to be. But he did it sometimes. And now he was beginning to be very effective.

It was obvious to the children that he was trying. And they liked him all the more for it.

The Father was already happy that he had decided to catch his children doing something right every now and then and to give them One Minute Praisings.

He reviewed in his mind how much they were like the last half of the One Minute Reprimand.

He found it useful to summarize what he'd learned to do:

One Minute Praisings work well when:

1. I tell my children ahead of time that I am going to praise them when they do something that makes me feel good.
   And I encourage them to do the same with me.

2. I catch my children doing something *right*.

3. I tell my children specifically what they *did*.

4. Then I tell them how good I *feel* about what they did and why it makes me feel so good.

5. I stop talking for a few seconds. The silence lets *them* feel the good feeling themselves.

6. Then I tell them that I *love* them.

7. I end the praising with a *hug*—or at least a light touch to let them know I care.

8. The Praising is short and sweet. When it's over, it's over.

9. I realize that it takes me only a minute to praise my children. But feeling good about themselves may last *them* for a lifetime.

10. I know that what I am doing is good for my children *and* for me. I feel really good about *myself*.

As the months went by, "The One Minute Father" (as his children now affectionately called him) really began to appreciate his youngsters.

And the children appeared to enjoy one another. They seemed to like themselves more than they ever had before.

The Father was glad he and his children were giving and receiving Reprimands and Praisings with all due respect to the other person. Everyone in the family, including The Father, felt better since the communications had improved.

They had become a happier family.

The Father sat in his living room one evening relaxing and thinking. Earlier in the evening, he had watched one of his youngsters doing her homework. It had started him thinking—about how people think.

The successful man knew from his work experience that people respond better when they are more involved. "But how," he wondered, "can my *children* get more involved in running their own lives?"

The Father knew if he could find a way, it would make life a lot easier—for them *and* for him.

Then he remembered something very basic.

*

GOALS
Begin
Behaviors

CONSEQUENCES
Maintain
Behaviors

*

The Father saw that he had emphasized the *consequences* of his children's behavior.

But as The Father thought about the happiest and most successful individuals he knew, he remembered one of the things they had in common—*goals*!

They knew what they wanted out of life.

He recalled, "Most of the people who succeed have a very clear idea of how they want to succeed, however they define success—love, money, peace of mind, whatever. They clearly know what they eventually want to have."

The financially successful man had studied the power of setting goals at work—although he had not considered applying it to his homelife.

He knew that most of the very highest achievers in the world—whether their achievements are physical, or financial, or artistic, or whatever— have written and specific goals.

The next highest group of achievers have goals but they are not written or specific. These people are also successful. But they realize only a fraction of what the top achievers experience.

The vast majority of people are not clear on what their goals are. And they experience a great deal less of what they would enjoy in life.

As The Father reviewed these facts, he recalled Pareto's Law. The sixteenth-century economist had observed that in Italy fewer than 20 percent of the people had more than 80 percent of the wealth, and as he looked at other nations, he found the same distribution, *regardless* of economic, political, or social structure.

"Today," The Father thought, "you can see the same phenomenon. A few people get most of the good things in life: emotional or physical love, good friends, financial security and so on.

"While it has been true for centuries, it seems a bit unfair," he mused, "that one person should get four pieces of the prosperity pie, while four people have to share the one piece that remains."

Just then, one of his daughters came into the living room and asked, "Can you help me with my English, Dad?" The girl was strong in math and science but not in the humanities. Two months ago she would have tried to bluff the answer. But now that she was gaining confidence, she was making a greater effort.

The Father spent the early part of the evening helping his daughter learn how to help herself.

When she left, he thought, "We are all stronger in some areas than in others."

The Father knew that in his own case he had been stronger in his work life than in his homelife. But he was changing that. He thought more about what he wanted for his children.

He knew he did not want them to be conforming, perfectly behaved little people. Too many children had had their spontaneous spirits broken in the name of "behaving themselves." He realized that some of the most interesting people in the world had been "difficult children."

The more he thought about it, the more fascinated he became. He looked closely at the word *behave*: behave . . . be-have . . . Be . . . Have.

"*Be* what?" he wondered. "*Have* what?

"I guess I want my children to be the kind of people they feel they can be. And to have a great attitude—about themselves and about life.

"A good attitude," The Father decided, "would be the greatest gift a parent could give a child."

Then The Father realized what he was doing. And he laughed—at himself. "Here I am trying to figure out what is good for them. They should be the ones doing this, not me."

The Father was interrupted again. It was his eldest daughter. "Dad, can we have the Wilsons over this weekend—just the kids?"

The Father thought of four more children in the house from Friday to Sunday night.

When she saw her father hesitating, she said, "It's important for us cousins to spend time together, Dad." The child knew which button to push. Dad was "into families" now.

The Father agreed to the visit. He liked his brother's children—sometimes. But nine children in the house? For the entire weekend?

By the time Friday night arrived, The Father was ready. As soon as the cousins arrived, he sat all the children down at the dining-room table and told them they were going to join him briefly for a "goal-setting meeting."

"All of us really want to enjoy this weekend. And neither you nor I want me to have to monitor you all the time. So I've got an idea. Everybody get a pencil and a piece of paper."

When they returned, the children were asked, "What do you want to have happen while you are together?"

The children all began to talk at once. The Father asked for quiet and said, "I want you to write down on a single sheet of paper what you each want from the weekend." They did. Then they went around the table and all of them read their lists of desires. They soon concluded they couldn't do that much in a year. They limited it to:

1. Have a lot of fun.
2. Stay up late one night and talk.
3. Make cookies and popcorn.
4. Go to a movie.
5. Go to the video arcade once.
6. Sleep outside one night.
7. Have a barbecue on the patio.

The Father said, "We have some of our goals now. The next is to agree. I'll speak for myself. I agree to all your goals except sleeping outside one night. The neighbors would really be upset with your noisy talking, yelling, and laughing."

One of the older children offered, "What if we agreed to talk quietly outside and go to sleep?"

"Then I'd agree to that," The Father responded. "So change that to 'sleep outside one night, talk quietly and go to sleep.' Please write it down."

They did. Then one of them asked, "You said we have 'some' of our goals. What are the others?"

The Father asked, "What would you like if you were the parent with nine children in your house?"

The children just looked at one another. They were silent for a few moments. Then one of the cousins said, "Be quiet when you're on the phone?" He had obviously heard that one at home.

"That's good. Please write it down—on the same sheet of paper."

The children came up with many other good ideas. Some of them were:

1. Be quiet when someone is on the phone.
2. Put away the sleeping bags.
3. Always clean up after ourselves.
4. Take out the garbage.
5. Wash the dishes.
6. Make our beds.
7. Share our things with each other.
8. Don't fight/Get along with each other.

"Congratulations," The Father said. "You have just created your own 'One Minute Goals.'"

"What?" several of them asked.

"You have just painted a mental picture of what you want to see happen. And you have done it very well. Your goals are attainable and very specific."

"Why are they called One Minute Goals?" the children wanted to know.

"I'll show you," The Father answered. "Read what you have written down. Then please turn your paper over. I am going to time you."

The younger children took a little longer but when they were finished, The Father said, "It took you only a minute or so to read your goals."

"Is that why they are called One Minute Goals?" one of the children asked.

"Yes. And for a very important reason." Then The Father suggested that they all write down the following words on the other side of their own pieces of paper:

*

I Take A Minute
I Look At My Goals
I Look At My Behavior

I See If My Behavior
Matches My Goals

*

"I get it," one of the cousins said. "You want us to take a minute and look at our goals—and then see if we're doing what we really wanted to do."

"That's almost exactly right!" The Father said.

"The more *often* we see in our minds what we want to have, the more likely we are to get it.

"However, let me correct one thing. Do I want you to get what you want? Or do you? Do I want you to take a minute to review your goals quickly or do *you*? Who are you really doing it for?"

The children laughed and said, "For ourselves."

The Father's older boy spoke up. "I think we should have our own meeting now and decide how we want to divide up the jobs. We can do it."

The Father never did see anything in writing about what they decided. But things went very well from that point on—at least most of the time.

The first night one of his sons and a cousin got a little loud as they "slept" outside. The Father called them in and gave them each a One Minute Reprimand in private. Then they behaved well.

On Saturday and Sunday mornings the man briefly gathered all the children together to let them review their own goals and behavior as a group. It was fun to listen to the discussion.

The Father was amused when he heard his children enthusiastically giving their cousins Praisings and Reprimands.

He sensed it wouldn't be long before the cousins began to give his children clear messages as well.

And he was happy for the youngsters, knowing that such communication leads to better relationships.

The weekend turned out, in fact, to be one of the most enjoyable any of them had spent in a good while. As the cousins left, saying thanks several times, The Father gave himself a Praising.

He had used One Minute Goals, Praisings, and Reprimands. He saw how well it worked.

After the successful weekend, The Father introduced his children to "I" goals.

"Remember how we set our goals together? Well, those were our 'We' goals—the goals that two or more members of the family agree on. Now how would you like to learn something that is strictly for your own benefit?"

"That would be great," they responded.

"Then just write down what you would like to see happen to you as though you were already doing something about it. Include when you would like to see it happen.

"For example, one of mine is 'I have good health. I am eating wisely and jog three miles a day by May fifth." It didn't take the children long to make up their own lists of goals. They included:

"I have become a cheerleader. I am practicing the routines every day. Final tryouts are March eleventh."

"I have good feelings about myself. I am catching myself doing something *right*. I feel good by May first."

As The Father saw his children's dreams on paper, he realized how quickly he and they were learning to enjoy a better life together.

He reviewed what they were doing:

One Minute Goals work well for our family when:

1. We have clear goals as a family ("We" goals), and as individuals ("I" goals).

2. We strive for mutual agreement so we all feel we are getting what we want from the family.

3. We each write out our goals in 250 words or fewer on a single piece of paper—so it takes us only a minute or so to reread them.

4. Our goals are *specific*, showing exactly what we would each like to see happen and when: "I have realized . . . I am doing . . . It has happened by . . ."

5. We each *reread* our goals often in order to make them mental habits—a way of thinking.

6. I take a minute out every now and then. I look at my own goals. I look at my behavior. I see if my behavior matches my goals.

7. I encourage my children to do the same.

8. Once a week, we enjoy reviewing our goals and progress together as a family.

Some of the children also had private goals—those they did not want to share with others. They were afraid that someone else might think they could never attain them. The Father respected this privacy.

Whatever the goals were, each child now felt more in control of his or her life. It wasn't just what the parent wanted that was important.

They began to assume some responsibility for running their own lives.

And they enjoyed it.

The little one had even gotten in on the act. She drew "pit tours" of what she wanted and called them her "golds."

The Father was pleased. It was no longer *his* system of One Minute Goals, One Minute Praisings, and One Minute Reprimands. It had become the children's system as well.

Life at home had become more enjoyable for The One Minute Father and his children. But that was not the case elsewhere.

 $\mathbf{M}$ EANWHILE, on the other side of town, another father—a younger man—and his wife were beginning to look at the way they were raising *their* children.

They had talked it over and they both agreed: Their two children were getting out of hand. Neither the nine- nor the six-year-old child listened to or was considerate of their parents. They were doing poorly in school and getting into skirmishes in the neighborhood.

The man didn't know how often the children's equally frustrated mother had said, "Just wait until your father comes home. You'll be sorry."

The children, threatened with his arrival, never knew that he thought he was just coming home "to his castle"—a peaceful fortress from the world.

He had enough challenges at work and longed for the peace and quiet of his own home. But all too often he was greeted with "I don't mean to bother you, honey, but do you know what the kids did today? I want you to do something about it! I just can't deal with it by myself."

The young couple knew that they didn't want their children to turn out like some of the other undisciplined youngsters who lived nearby, who ran roughshod over their parents and everyone else.

So the young man spanked his children. And when that didn't work, he tried spanking them harder. But he did not feel good about what he was doing.

He reminded himself of the joke about the man who threatened his son with "If I see you hit your little brother once more, I'll hit you so hard . . ."

As the couple looked around at the other parents in the neighborhood, they became more discouraged. It seemed to them that many other parents were in the same boat—a leaky one at that. They were confused, not knowing how much freedom to allow or how much control to apply.

No one had ever told them how to be parents. The truth was that they had never thought much about raising children. But they knew they needed to learn.

The young man expressed his frustration. Other men in the neighborhood agreed. "It's not like it used to be," many of them said. "Things are changing so fast that just when we learn the rules, they change the rules on us. Who knows what our families want from us?"

The man understood all too well how so many of the other fathers felt. In a way he was relieved to learn that he was not the only one.

The younger father's situation continued to grow worse. The problems he and his wife were having with their children put a stress on the marriage.

And as his life at home became more unpleasant, it began to affect his work.

Finally, he sought professional help. He heard the advice of marriage and family counselors, psychiatrists, social workers, pediatricians, and psychologists. He learned useful "bits and pieces" from many of them. But he was still confused.

T HEN a good friend told the young father about a man who lived in his neighborhood. After going through a difficult time himself, this man was apparently raising five marvelous children.

The best part of all was that he had developed a simple and effective parenting method which was easy to learn. And the man was willing to share it with other parents. The young man telephoned and introduced himself.

"To tell you the truth, I'm pretty confused. I would really appreciate it, sir, if I could come over and talk with you about being a father."

"Certainly," the older man said. "Why don't you come Saturday morning. I'd be glad to help.

"That is," he added, "on one condition."

Then The One Minute Father laughed and said, "It's nothing to worry about, I assure you. It's just that what I will tell you is so simple that it is hard for some people to believe how well it works.

"So I would just ask you to wait before you pass any judgment on it until you have tried it in your own home for a few weeks."

The young father agreed.

On Saturday morning, as the younger man drove up to the impressive house, he thought, "This man is obviously successful. No wonder he is a good father. He's probably smarter than me. He . . ."

The young man paused and then he stopped putting himself down, remembering that his own father had done enough of that long ago. He wanted to change.

The younger father was greeted at the front door by a gray-haired man who seemed physically fit and whose bright eyes gave the impression of someone in the midst of a happy life.

"Come in," the older man said. "I'm glad you came over to see me."

"You are?" the surprised young man responded.

"Yes. Frankly, I'm pleased that someone else is just as confused as I was—and just as keen to learn how to do better. And that was not so long ago!"

"You? You were in the same situation?"

The Father smiled and said, "I knew a good deal about some things but not much about fathering. As Will Rogers said, 'We are *all* ignorant. We are just ignorant about different things.'"

The younger man began to relax.

He slowly admitted his greatest fear. "I don't know. . . . I'm afraid I have to do things just right or I'll harm my children. Sometimes I think you have to be perfect to be a good parent."

The Father started to laugh. Then he said with a smile, "Fortunately, nothing could be further from the truth. Every father is going to make mistakes, just as he does with many other parts of his life. And his children are going to know it, too."

"So what do you do," the young man asked, "when you make a mistake?"

"I used to try to cover it up. But the first thing I do now is admit it. My children really appreciate it when I can admit to making a mistake.

"It means they can do the same with me.

"And next, if the mistake is not a terrible one—and most aren't—I let myself laugh about it."

"Laugh about it?" the astonished man asked.

"Yes! Laugh at your own human follies and you teach your child to laugh at his.

"Anyone who can be honest enough to admit quickly that he was wrong and then laugh at his own imperfections will never have a nervous breakdown."

The young man nodded and said, "It sounds like a great way to take a lot of stress out of life."

"It is," The Father said. "And another way to reduce stress is not to wait for large blocks of time—time enough to do things just right.

"There never seems to be enough time to do everything you want to do—let alone time enough to do it just right. And that includes the time required to be a good father."

The younger man nodded his head in agreement and asked, "So what's the answer?"

"Let me say, first of all," The One Minute Father cautioned, "that I do not have all the answers to raising children. I'm simply fortunate enough to know a few small things that you or any other parent can learn, and they will make a big difference.

"There are probably as many answers to raising children," The Father said, "as there are parents.

"However, a point of view that I find useful is this:

*

*I Simply
Let My Children Know
By The Way I Treat Them*

*That I Am Glad
They Are
Who They Are*

*

"That's very good," the young man reflected.

The Father suggested, "Rather than give you 'the answers,' why don't I just tell you what I do and then you can adapt it in the way you feel will work best for you and your family."

"Fine," the younger man said. "I'm listening."

"Before I tell you what I do, however, you should know that I don't always do it."

"What?" the surprised visitor said.

The Father shrugged his shoulders and admitted, "I'm like any other parent. I don't always do what I know I should do.

"But when I do, things are a lot better.

"First let me tell you that I no longer worry about the amount of time I spend on parenting. I just make sure that, balanced with the other responsibilities and enjoyments I have in life, I do try to spend as much time as I can with each of my children."

The visitor smiled and said, "I'm glad to hear that. When I first heard that they called you The One Minute Father, I got the impression that you might rush through whatever you did with your children. And that, in fact, you spent very little time with them."

The Father returned the smile. "You are right to be concerned about such a possibility.

"The important thing to know is this:

"Since I have learned to use a simple three-part communication system—which takes me no longer than a minute at a time to use—literally *every* minute I spend with my children has been enhanced.

"But before I tell you about the three specific methods of communication, let me say first that I spend time *alone* with each child—even if it's only for a few minutes—and I never compare one child to another. And second, I am totally *present*. I try to concentrate fully on whichever son or daughter I am with at the moment."

"So you really stay in the present moment."

"Yes. When I am at home now I think only about my homelife. And when I am at work I think only about my work. It is a big help in *both* areas!"

The visitor said, "Yes, my friend told me that you are becoming as successful at home as you have been elsewhere. That must make you feel pretty good."

"It does," The Father said with some pride. "Especially because my children are experiencing the same feelings of success.

"It has been easier on all of us since I have realized that:

*

*My Two Main Goals
As A Parent Are
To Help My Children Gain*

*SELF-ESTEEM
And
SELF-DISCIPLINE*

*

"And in *that* order," The Father added.

"I have learned the painful way that children who like and appreciate who they are (that is, who have self-esteem) develop self-discipline—as a favor to *themselves*.

"If they like themselves enough, they will want to take care of themselves. And one of the best ways anyone can do that is by developing self-discipline."

"Is that," the younger father asked, "what the three One Minute methods of communication do for children?"

"Almost," The Father responded. "It's more what they help children do for themselves."

Then he added, "In fact, my children are now using these same three methods to communicate with me and with each other."

At the visitor's request, The Father described in detail One Minute Goals, Praisings, and Reprimands.

The younger man listened intently.

Then he said slowly, "Maybe that would work for me."

"You don't sound too sure," The Father commented.

"I'm *not* sure," the visitor said.

"Maybe it would help me if I could understand *why* the three communication methods work so well for parents.

"Just why *do* One Minute Goals, One Minute Praisings, and One Minute Reprimands help children 'like themselves and behave themselves'?"

"YOU want to know why One Minute Goals work so well with children.

"Let's begin," The Father suggested, "by looking at how the human mind works. Most scientists recognize that the mind has two parts."

"The conscious mind," the younger man interjected, "and the subconscious mind . . . the part that is aware and the part that is unaware."

"Right. And the powerful part of the mind is the subconscious. We may not be aware of it but it is recording everything that it sees and hears.

"The most amazing thing is that the subconscious mind has no filter on it. It lets in anything and everything. It is the basis for our beliefs. Anything that goes into our subconscious often enough tends to become a belief."

"Like whatever we are frequently told as children," the young man said, "we tend to believe—even if we may not think it is true."

"That's exactly the point. You probably know children who have been told they were stupid or clumsy. They come to believe that it is true."

The young man remembered his own childhood. "And then they act as though it were true."

"Yes," The Father said. "And when children act as though something is true . . ."

". . . it becomes true," the young man completed.

"And that," The Father said, "is the basis for why One Minute Goals work so well—because this is an easy way for people to put what they want into their subconscious minds—over and over again—until they believe it.

"And, as we said, when you believe it, you will act as though it were true."

"What if the goals are unrealistic?" the young man wanted to know.

"That's the beautiful part of the system. The subconscious has no filter. It lets everything in. It doesn't know what's realistic and what isn't. Only the conscious mind functions on that level."

"I'm not sure I understand," the younger man admitted.

"Let me give you an analogy," The Father said.

"Imagine a farmer planting seeds in the soil. The fertile soil is very like the subconscious mind. It doesn't care what kind of seed you plant— nutritious, like corn and wheat, or poisonous— deadly nightshade, for example. The soil will grow whatever you plant. It doesn't care."

The young man saw the point. "And so will our subconscious minds."

"Exactly! Now you understand why One Minute Goals work so well."

"Because . . ." the younger father said slowly, "you can read and reread your goals in only a minute . . . which is a convenient way to repeatedly put them into your subconscious mind . . . and thus you come to believe them . . . and eventually to act on them."

"That's a marvelous capsule explanation of why One Minute Goals are so effective—with children and with ourselves."

"Is that all there is to it?"

"Not quite," The Father said with a smile.

"But a good focus for now is:

*

We Become

What We
Think About

*

"That is a terrific thought!" the young man said. "I think I'm going to use it myself!"

"Interesting you should say that," The Father said with a smile. The visitor looked puzzled.

The Father admitted, "Of all the things I've learned in the recent past, that is one of the most important. Remember that I said that I was not as successful at home as I was elsewhere? Well, take an educated guess *why*."

The young man was embarrassed. He didn't know what to say. He was amazed that the older man could be so vulnerable. "I gather it has something to do with what we are talking about."

"Yes. It does."

"Could it simply be that you didn't have a happy homelife because it wasn't one of your goals?"

"As amazing as it may sound, that is precisely right. I had taken it for granted. As if it were my right—my reward for working so hard at my job."

The younger father knew the feeling.

"I've solved that problem now," The Father said. "I have my own 'family life' goals clearly written down. I refer to them frequently. And, of course, the more often I see them, the more apt I am to achieve them.

"I think of this as my 'popcorn principle.'"

"What?" the young man asked.

The Father laughed. "You may have heard of the experiment they did in movie theaters—until it was outlawed. They flashed a picture of buttered popcorn on the screen and the words BUY POPCORN.

"It came off and on so fast no one saw it."

"But I'll bet," the younger father figured out, "that people's subconscious minds 'saw' it, right?"

"That's exactly right! And guess what?"

The visitor said, "They sold a lot of popcorn!"

"And that's the whole point. The subconscious mind has a positive influence on our behavior. Unfortunately, the opposite is also true.

"For example, a couple of Saturdays ago, I was reading the sports section of the paper. A pro golfer, who was leading at the end of three rounds, was quoted. He said, 'I'm a scarecrow golfer.'

"When the reporter asked him what he meant, he said, 'I scare a lot of the big guys.'"

"In other words," the young father said, "he thought of himself as *almost* winning. He saw himself as only 'scaring' the best golfers in the game—just giving them a close call."

"Sure. The next day I looked at the paper. Guess what he shot the last day of the tournament."

The visitor shook his head from side to side, afraid of what the answer would be.

The Father said, "Of course. He shot a seventy-six—just high enough to finish out of the big money.

"You don't win by thinking about losing."

Then The Father looked at his watch. "It's almost time."

"Time for what?" the younger father inquired.

"Our family's Saturday morning gathering. The children are aware of your visit and have agreed that you may join us for part of it if you like."

The young father eagerly joined the children in the dining room. He wasn't sure what to expect.

T HE visitor was surprised to see that the children ran a good deal of the meeting.

They reviewed their Goals, individually and as a family, and they gave one another Praisings and Reprimands. There was a good deal of good-natured kidding and laughing. But there was no doubt that these five children were beginning to run their own lives—and with some success.

Toward the end of the meeting, the older boy said, "You know how one of our goals is to take care of each other?

"Well, I read where one hundred and fifty thousand kids are kidnapped every year. They say having fingerprints on record would help identify a lost child. Why don't we make fingerprints of baby sis's fingers?"

"How?" one of the others asked.

"We'll just get an ink pad and an index card and do it ourselves. We'll keep the card here at home."

One of the girls put her hand on his arm and said, "'Big Bro,' you obviously care about little sis. And you've come up with a really good idea. I want you to know how good that makes me feel!"

The children broke into mock applause for the Praising. But it was easy to tell they meant it.

"Let's do it for all the kids in the family," one of them suggested.

Everyone agreed. After the meeting broke up, the children left for the local stationery store to put their plan into action.

"That's amazing!" the visitor said.

"A few short months ago, I would have thought it was amazing, too," The Father admitted. "But that's what's happened since I started catching my children doing something *right*—or even approximately right.

"You can't believe the difference it has made in each of my children!"

"So *why* do you think the One Minute Praisings work so well?" the visitor wanted to know.

"Because, more than any other thing I know, the feedback they receive helps them feel good about themselves.

"All too often, I used to forget to recognize my children when they were doing well."

The young father smiled and said, "I saw a great cartoon about that recently.

"It shows Dennis the Menace sitting in the corner, with a tear in his eye. And he says, 'How come I don't have a special place to sit when I do something NICE?'" The Father laughed.

"Now that I think of it," the younger father said, "I don't give *my* children much attention either when they are behaving well."

"Believe me," The Father assured his visitor, "when you do, it will be a great help to them.

"If you want to help your children develop quickly, just remember '*Feedback* is the breakfast of champions.'

"And the best feedback is one the children can see for themselves."

*

*The Best Way For
Children To Believe
They Are Winners*

*Is For Them To
See Themselves
Winning!*

*

"The greatest example of this," the Father said, "is the absolutely true story about the father who set things up so his small son would win— regardless of what the child did."

The younger father laughed. "It sounds like the boy is going to grow into a real winner!"

"Of course he is!" The One Minute Father responded.

"How did the father do it?" the visitor asked.

"He taught his son how to bowl—like a lot of other fathers. However, he did things differently than most of us do with our children.

"He had the automatic pin machine set up the ten bowling pins as usual. Then, to his friends' amazement, the father set up several additional pins. He placed them at the end of the gutter."

"At the end of the gutter?" the astonished young father asked. "You did say *the gutter*?"

"Yes," the older man replied.

"Of course we both know that when you throw the ball so badly that it goes in the gutter, you get a zero score—because you miss all the pins."

"So why did he do it?" asked the young man.

"I'll answer your question by asking you one. Knowing that the boy was just learning and that he was only four years old, where do you think the little guy was going to throw the ball?"

The young father smiled. "I'm afraid he's going to throw it in the gutter."

"Sure. And most of us fathers would be literally 'afraid' of the same thing.

"But this father didn't care where his son's ball went. He always moved the pins in front of the ball."

The young man laughed. "I love it!"

"Isn't that great? No matter where the small fry threw the ball, he was a 'winner'!"

The young man nodded his head and smiled.

"When the young man grew up, what do you think he became—other than a winner, which he did do?"

"A professional bowler?"

"You guessed it. A very prosperous professional bowler! In fact, many years later, after winning more money than any other bowler on the tour, he was asked what his key to success was. Nelson Burton spoke about his father with pride.

"'I don't ever remember missing,' he said. 'I had an unusual dad!'"

Both men quietly thought about what they had just heard. Each would like to have had such a father himself.

Now they wanted be like that for their children.

The younger father said, "That story reminds me of what another father did for another little boy. To help his young son learn to play basketball, he encouraged the youngster to drop little tennis balls into a big wastepaper basket. Again, 'the kid couldn't miss.'

"It's funny, though, how I never thought of doing something like that for *my* son," he confessed.

The One Minute Father smiled and said, "Somehow I think you're going to.

"And the more you do, the more you will bring out the best in your child."

"Is that why catching a child doing something right works so well?" the young father asked. "Because it brings out the good that is already there?"

"That's exactly why it works. Each of us is capable of using good judgment and making good decisions—if we are rewarded for doing so."

"Why do you think that children have this inherent wisdom within them?" the young man asked.

"Because you can see it every day. Just watch children live their lives. Like us, they do very well when they learn to trust what their gut is telling them.

"In fact, there was once an interesting study that illustrates just how well children know what is best for them.

"A special cafeteria was set up in a school, one that was divided into two halves. One half had all the goodies—ice cream, pizza, candy, et cetera.

"The other side of the cafeteria was stocked with equally attractive items but these were more nourishing foods—the kind the children were often told they were 'supposed' to eat.

"Then the social scientists who were doing this study told the children, 'You may eat in this cafeteria every day. You may choose anything you want. And it won't cost you or your parents anything.'"

"That," the young man said, "sounds like a pretty good deal."

The One Minute Father smiled and said, "Sure. Now what do you think happened the first day the children descended on that cafeteria?"

The young father replied, "If they are anything like my two children, they ate all the junk they could get their hands on!"

"That's exactly what happened."

"And what do you think happened on the second day?"

"The same thing," the young father answered.

"Essentially, yes," The Father confirmed.

"But by the end of the second week, what do you think the children did?

"Remember," The Father cautioned, "they still had the right to eat whatever food and as much food as they wanted."

The young father said, "I don't know. What *did* happen?"

"Long lines started to form on the nutritious side of the cafeteria. Most of the children grew sick of the junk food and wanted healthier foods. They chose what was good for them!

"Left to their own good judgment, most of the children behaved in that cafeteria the way they behave in life. They know what is good for them and they will choose it.

"The problem is," The One Minute Father said, "most parents don't believe they will."

"So," the younger father interjected, "we act as if they won't."

"Exactly. And then guess what happens."

"The children make bad decisions," the young father began to realize, "and we have to keep 'straightening them out.'"

"Yes, and that, as you probably have found out for yourself, is exhausting for any father."

"So that's why," the young father said with sudden understanding, "giving children One Minute Praisings works so well.

"They help children see that they are winners— that they have good judgment and that they can do almost anything well—if they just rely on their own good instincts.

"I know that neither you nor I wants frightened well-behaved robots for children," The Father said.

"I want my children to have the kind of judgment that leads them to behave themselves not because they have to but because they want to—because they discover that it really helps them be whatever *they* believe they can be.

"Walt Disney once described the kind of child perhaps many of us would like to have been or at least to have in our own family—the kind of confident, free spirit that is so rare today.

"Mr. Disney used to like to tell his friends: 'Remember the story about the boy who wanted to march in a circus parade? When the show came to town, the bandmaster needed a trombonist, so the boy signed up. He hadn't marched a block before the fearful noises from his horn caused two old ladies to faint and a horse to run away. The bandmaster demanded, "Why didn't you tell me you couldn't play the trombone?" And the boy said, "How did I know? I never tried before!"'"

The young man laughed.

"Then," The Father continued, "Mr. Disney added, 'Many years ago I might have done just what that boy did. Now I'm a grandfather and have a good many gray hairs and what a lot of people call common sense. But if I'm no longer young in age, I hope I stay young enough in spirit never to fear failure—young enough to take a chance and march in the parade.'"

The Father thought for a moment and then said, "I really would like my children to think like that. I wish I had done it more myself as a child."

"What you are saying, as I understand it, is that you set things up for your children to win. And if they can't see for themselves that they are winning, then you tell them when *you* see it. Hence the use of the One Minute Praisings."

"You have a great gift for crystalizing your thoughts," The Father said. "Let me add just one more practical point. I've learned that the more I give my children Praisings, rather than Reprimands, the better the outcome is."

The younger father thought about what he had heard. Then he said, "What you've learned from your experiences with your children reminds me of the lesson in the Wind and the Sun parable."

"What lesson?" The Father wanted to know.

The young father had noticed that The One Minute Father was always keen to learn more.

"The Wind and the Sun were having an argument," the younger man said, "about which was the stronger force in the universe.

"The Wind was boasting that it was clearly the more powerful force. It pointed out that it had uprooted trees and destroyed whole towns when it gathered itself into a hurricane. It said it could toss ships at sea and send them to the bottom of the ocean. *It* was the more powerful force!

"The Sun said quietly, 'Perhaps you are.'

"The Wind wouldn't let it go at that. He said, 'Of course I'm more powerful. And I'll prove it. Let's you and me, Sun, have a contest and we'll settle this.' The Sun agreed.

"The Wind looked around and said, 'See that old man walking on the road below? Well, let's just see who is stronger. I'll soon blow his coat and hat away! Watch this!'

"The Sun hid her smile. And the Wind began to blow. As the winds came up, the old man grabbed his hat off his head and held it in his hand. The winds increased. And the old man drew his coat around him more tightly. The more the wind blew, the more tightly the old man clung to his hat and coat.

"The Wind blew hard for ten minutes.

"Finally the Wind gave up.

"Then the Sun emerged from behind a cloud.

"As the Sun came out, the man began to get warm. He looked up immediately, and squinted. The Sun grew very hot. Within five minutes, the man was so hot . . ."

The One Minute Father laughed and finished the sentence, ". . . the man took off his coat!"

"Exactly," the younger father said.

Then the young man added with a grin, "And it took only a very few *minutes* to get the results!"

"I like this story," The One Minute Father said, enjoying the obvious reference to a quicker way of getting good results.

"I thought you would," the young man said. "Speaking of getting good results quickly," he added, "can we go on to One Minute Reprimands?"

"Certainly," The Father responded.

"In fact," The One Minute Father admitted, "that parable reminds me of the way I used to 'blow' at my children. By that, I mean how I used to talk to them, in one form or another, so that they felt I thought that *they* were bad.

"And of course, the harder I 'blew,' the more they 'hung on' to their bad behavior."

"That's what I don't understand," the younger father said. "You say that you give your children One Minute Reprimands and that it has helped. I would have thought they would backfire on you. Why *do* One Minute Reprimands work so well?"

"**O**NE Minute Reprimands work because they help me give my children what they need most—discipline and love—*when* they need it.

"Reprimands provide me with a practical way to deal with problems when they arise—and as you well know, they always arise.

"I know it is wise not to tolerate intolerable behavior," The Father said. "And so I never have—at work or at home. However, when it came to my children, I just made things worse."

"That's how it still is at my house," the younger father said. "I don't think I should have to tolerate intolerable behavior either.

"However, not only does my children's behavior not improve, but both they and my wife seem to resent me for trying to do something about it."

"Let me suggest," The One Minute Father said, "that they probably resent the *way* you do it."

The One Minute Father smiled and added, "The situation you are still in reminds me of myself."

"You?" the young man said.

"Yes. I used to 'howl like the wind.' I yelled at them for doing wrong. And then I punished them."

"But it didn't work?" the younger father asked.

"No. It just made things worse."

"Now I've learned that people all react pretty much the same way. It doesn't make any difference if it is you or your wife or your children, or me or my children. None of us likes to be yelled at or put down as a person.

"And that is one of the most important reasons *why* the Reprimand works so well. Because:

*

*When I Use
The One Minute Reprimand*

*My Children
Feel Bad
About Their Behavior
But Good
About Themselves*

*

"Is it all right for the children to feel bad?"

"As long as it is only about their behavior, yes.

"In fact, I *want* them to feel bad about that part of the encounter with me," The Father said.

Just then, the men heard a car pull up. The children had returned from their trip to the stationery store. The Father's seven-year-old daughter came in and said, "Excuse me, Dad. But will it bother you if I skateboard outside?"

The One Minute Father said, "No, honey. But it *is* wet outside. So think about what you are doing. And take care of yourself."

The two men returned to their conversation.

"So you believe that children should experience the consequences of their behavior."

"Absolutely!" The Father said. "The Reprimand works because it is an unpleasant consequence which occurs as a result of unacceptable behavior.

"From what I have learned about discipline— from the many professional people I spoke with and from my own personal experiences with my children—the best discipline is *unpleasant* and *educational*.

"If it is only one or the other, it won't work."

"I made it *unpleasant*," the young man said. Then he laughed. "At least I was good at *part* of it."

The Father laughed too. "You're starting to become a One Minute Father, aren't you?"

"What do you mean?" the young man asked.

"You're beginning to laugh a little at your own mistakes. It takes a lot of stress out of parenting.

"You wanted to know why the Reprimand works so much better. Let me tell you:

*

I Provide
Loving
Discipline

As A Gift
To My Children

*

"The key word is *loving*," The Father noted.

"More than any other reason, the One Minute Reprimand works because it shows my children how much I love and care about them.

"When I limit my comments specifically to what my child *did* and how I feel about it—and do so in only about half a minute or so—I am loving my child. I do not go on and on about it. I say it is the *behavior* I am disappointed with—not my child.

"It is an act of love to stop reprimanding, to catch my breath, to calm down, and to remember that I want to *support* my child. I want to back up my son or daughter all the way."

The younger man listened. He sensed some of what this man's children must feel.

"It is the *last* half of the Reprimand that is so powerful. When I remind my children that they are better people than that kind of behavior shows, I am telling them how highly I really think of them.

"It was hard for me to do at first—especially when I was angry," The Father said, "but telling my children that I love them—even when they have made a serious mistake—has made all the difference in the world! My family now—"

The Father was interrupted by the sound of crying outside the window. His little girl had fallen.

The Father jumped up and looked out. His daughter was getting up slowly. She was bleeding slightly but she seemed to be OK. He sat down and waited for her to come in. The visitor was surprised. The Father seemed not to care.

The little girl came in crying. The Father said nothing. He let her cry. When she finished, The Father asked, "Are you OK?"

"Yes," she said. "I hit my elbow but not bad."

The Father did not hug her or comfort her. He simply asked, "Would you like to go skateboarding again, honey—on wet concrete without elbow pads?"

The visitor thought The Father was being far too tough. He would have run out and picked up his daughter and taken care of her.

The little girl said quietly, "No."

Her father asked, "No? What are you going to do next time?" The little girl just looked at the floor.

Then her dad smiled, looked at her with a gleam in his eye, and asked, "Are you sure you wouldn't like to go back out and maybe skateboard some more on the wet concrete with no pads on to protect you?"

The little girl started to smile and then she began to laugh through the traces of tears. "No, Dad. That would be dumb!"

"That's right! And you're not dumb. You're smart." Then The Father and the little girl hugged each other and she left.

The One Minute Father breathed a sigh of relief. "Thank God she wasn't hurt."

The visitor said, "Frankly, at first I thought you were a bit callous. You didn't take care of her the way one should take care of a little girl."

"You're right," The Father agreed. "I didn't. I did something far more valuable. I helped her learn more about taking care of herself.

"I think the sooner we each learn to take good care of ourselves, the better. One of the things I want most for my children is what I want for myself. To develop good judgment."

The Father explained. "I try to let my children learn through their own valuable experiences just as I was fortunate enough to learn through mine.

"I treat my sons and daughters in essentially the same way—that is, I feel that all of them can do whatever they believe they can do, and that none of them needs to be protected. In short, I treat them as though they were capable young people.

"In those rare instances when I feel they cannot see for themselves what they are doing wrong, then I give them a One Minute Reprimand.

"The Reprimand is simply another way for them to experience the pain of their mistakes—early and safely in the privacy of their home.

"The Reprimand works," The Father said, "because it helps me catch things easily *right away*—very soon after my children first get off course."

"Like NASA's monitoring system," the younger father said, "for the *Apollo* landing on the moon."

"What do you mean?" The One Minute Father asked.

"The *Apollo* spacecraft that carried American astronauts to the moon was off course most of the time," the younger father explained.

"Is that true?" The One Minute Father asked.

The young man nodded and The Father said, "That's amazing—when you consider that it completed its mission successfully. I can still remember how proud I was that we Americans were the first people to land on the moon.

"But I don't understand what that has to do with the One Minute Reprimand."

"The key to *Apollo*'s success was that it was monitored almost constantly. The moment it got a few degrees off course, it was put back on track."

"So," The Father said, "the spacecraft was never allowed to get very far off course."

"Precisely," the younger father said. "Therefore, they never had any big problems. Because they always solved the problems when they were easy."

It was enjoyable for the younger father to be sharing his knowledge with the older man. Somehow he felt smarter in this man's company. He was beginning to realize how wise he could be.

As the young father listened to himself, he thought about how that applied to parenting.

The Father was quiet, knowing that the young man was thinking. Then he said, "You seem to know about catching problems when they are small."

Then he smiled and added, "And you're asking *me* why the One Minute Reprimand works so well?"

He asked the young man, "Do you remember what I told you when we first met? That you just didn't know you already knew the answers? That you were not yet using what you intuitively knew?

"Well, you just demonstrated for us what I meant.

"Over the centuries many other men and women have done a good job of raising children.

"In various ways, such good parents instinctively do pretty much the same thing: They make it clear what they expect, they praise their youngsters, and they soon let them know when they are out of line—*without* beating them up.

"The One Minute Reprimand works because it is so compatible with something that is very important:

*

*What's Important
Is Not What I Think
About My Children*

It's What My Children
Believe
About Themselves

*

Then The Father posed a series of interesting questions. "What if each of my children believes that he or she is indeed a good and worthwhile person? What if they have a nonviolent way to express their anger or frustration with another person safely and effectively—such as the kind of Reprimand we have been talking about?"

"And by nonviolent," The Father said, "I mean one that does not attack another person.

"How likely do you think it is that they will become a problem for society? Are such people likely to become violent criminals? Are they likely to start a war? Or to attack people in other ways?"

The young man answered, "No. I think they would have a sense of peace within themselves."

"I would agree with you," The Father said. "However, what do you see so many parents do to their children—say in a supermarket?"

The young father said, "If you mean when a child misbehaves, I guess I've seen a number of different reactions from parents. But the ones I remember most are the parents who yell and tell the child that he is bad or hit him or threaten to leave him in the market."

"Exactly," The Father agreed. "Now we all lose our patience with our children now and then, but can you imagine how we must look to a small child? It would be like one of us looking up at someone twenty feet tall who is verbally abusing us.

"If the store manager saw that going on between two adults, he'd call the police. But what do we do when it happens to a defenseless child?"

"Nothing." The young father winced. "I'm afraid I've yelled at my own children and carried it too far."

The Father said, "We all have. I remember, before I started to use the Reprimand as my only method of discipline, how resentful my older son and I were. I had kept a lot of frustrations buried inside me, and then every once in a while they would erupt and strike out. And it wasn't long before my boy was striking back.

"We wonder why so many kids are angry. Violent crimes are highest among juveniles."

"That reminds me," the younger father said, "of what a warden said recently on television. The prison official, who sees things firsthand, said, 'When we have fewer violated children we will have fewer violent criminals.'"

The Father didn't speak. He thought about what he had just heard. And about what might have happened if he hadn't learned a better way to treat his children. No one ever thought it could happen to him, of course, but . . .

"So what you are saying," the young man continued, "is that the benefits of this nonviolent method of discipline are twofold. It can make a difference in our society because if enough people begin to use it or another method similar to it, we will have fewer angry juveniles."

"And if we use it in our own homes, we will benefit from the improved attitude and behavior of our own children. The Reprimand works because it is part of a communication system.

"Setting One Minute Goals, giving One Minute Praisings, and applying One Minute Reprimands all contribute to making children feel good about themselves."

"I'm beginning to think," the young father said, "that the same three parenting methods would work very well in *my* home."

"They will!" The Father assured him.

"You just need to do what you now know works. It is a challenge to change your behavior—to break old habits—but it is rewarding when you do.

"And remember," The One Minute Father added, "that these three methods of personal communication with your children are just a slice of the parenting pie. Being a good parent takes a good deal more than spending a minute now and then with your children. Nonetheless, the One Minute communication method will be a great help to you.

"And as far as all the rest goes," The Father offered, "you might want to remember the one simple rule of thumb I use. It will help you in a variety of ways."

"What is that?" the young father wanted to know.

"I try to treat my children the same way I expect to be treated."

The visitor said, "I think now I know why the One Minute Reprimand works so well. It is really just the golden rule: 'Do unto others as you would have others do unto you.'

"All of us," the younger man noted, "make mistakes. And I guess we all want someone who really loves us to tell us when our behavior is unattractive and yet remind us that *we* are valued."

To the visitor's surprise, he heard the mock sound of a roaring airplane drawing near. It preceded The Father's younger son into the den. "Can I interrupt you for a minute, Dad?"

The Father agreed. He quickly fixed the model airplane so his son could fly it again.

The boy left with "Thanks, Dad." Then The Father turned to his visitor and said, "You know, you and I are a lot like my boy's model plane."

"How is that?" the visitor asked.

"We are models for our sons and daughters. They watch us more than they listen to us.

"And one of the things they see when they see us get angry or sad (or whatever else we are feeling) during a Reprimand, is that it is OK for a person to express feelings." He added with a smile, "Even a man."

"So," the young father said, "there are many reasons why such a seemingly simple thing as a One Minute Reprimand is so effective.

"Children can learn a good deal about more than their behavior. They can learn about themselves."

"You're learning," The Father said.

He was pleased that the young man had come to see him.

The young man slowly shook his head and said, "I just don't know . . . if I can do it. It's hard for me to touch the people I care about and actually to come out and say, 'I love you.'"

The Father laughed and replied, "I didn't say it was easy!" He thought for a moment. "I remember when I first began to use One Minute Parenting, I was very apprehensive.

"All of a sudden, I was the only parent in the house. Two of my five children were teenagers—a boy and a girl. They were uncomfortable, with me and with themselves. I didn't know what to do."

"What *did* you do?" the visitor asked.

The One Minute Father smiled and said, "I looked at the alternatives."

"Which were?" the young man asked.

"You tell me," The Father responded. "What are *your* choices?"

"Well, I guess either to do nothing, to keep doing things the same way I am now, or . . . to change—to do something new."

"How," The Father asked, "do you think things will turn out with your wife and children if you do either of your first two alternatives?"

The young father laughed. "Not so good."

"So what's your choice?" The Father asked.

The young man thought for several moments. Then he said quietly, "I think I'm going to give it a try."

The One Minute Father leaned forward and said in a loud and crisp voice, "WHAT?"

The younger father laughed out loud. "I guess I was being a little timid," he said, "wasn't I?"

The One Minute Father said, "Take the pressure off yourself. Don't try to do things *just right*. Don't worry about making mistakes. You're going to make them. The important thing is to *do* what you now know!"

The younger father stood up and shook hands with the older man. He thanked him, promised he'd let him know how things went, and left.

IT was early evening when the young father arrived home. His wife asked anxiously, "Well, dear, what did you find out?"

The young father smiled. "You won't believe it. At least I didn't at first. He just told me what I already knew. But he's organized the knowledge into three very simple ways for parents to communicate with their children. And apparently it works wonders!"

The woman smiled and said, "I'll believe it works when I see it for myself. But if it's about communicating better, I'd like to know more."

They made a pot of coffee together and talked well into the night. The young mother thought that it all made a lot of good sense. In some ways, it was what she and her husband had been talking about themselves.

They just weren't clear how to go about it.

"I do have one big problem, however, with the whole idea," the mother said.

"The idea of a One Minute Father or One Minute Mother seems wrong. Parents should spend more than a minute with their children."

The young father agreed. "That's exactly what the One Minute Father said to me as I was leaving. The system just frees us up to do all the other important things we want to do with our children. And that's just what I want to do."

The woman thought for a moment. "In that case, I like it." Then she looked at her husband and added, "And it may leave more time for *us*."

The very next day the young father began to practice what he had learned. It was not easy in the beginning. He felt awkward. And his children did not always understand. But with his wife's participation and support, the inevitable happened.

He became a One Minute Father not because of what he knew but because of what he *did*.

He set One Minute Goals.

He gave One Minute Praisings.

He applied One Minute Reprimands.

He hugged his children, spoke the simple truth, expressed his feelings clearly, and laughed at his own mistakes.

And perhaps most important of all, he encouraged his children to do the same.

He even created a "Game Plan" summary of One Minute Parenting. He gave a copy to each of his children—just to remind him and them that while life was a priceless adventure to be valued and respected, it was also a game to be enjoyed.

THE ONE MINUTE FATHER'S "GAME PLAN"

*I Teach My Children to Like Themselves
and to Like to Behave Themselves.
And I Enjoy Myself in the Process.*

- I set goals, and praise and reprimand behavior.
- I speak the simple truth and express my feelings clearly.
- I hug my children and laugh often.

AND I ENCOURAGE MY CHILDREN TO DO AS I DO.

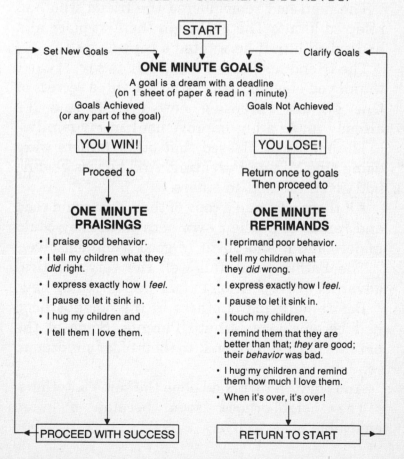

START

Set New Goals — Clarify Goals

ONE MINUTE GOALS

A goal is a dream with a deadline
(on 1 sheet of paper & read in 1 minute)

Goals Achieved
(or any part of the goal)

Goals Not Achieved

YOU WIN!

YOU LOSE!

Proceed to

Return once to goals
Then proceed to

**ONE MINUTE
PRAISINGS**

**ONE MINUTE
REPRIMANDS**

- I praise good behavior.
- I tell my children what they *did* right.
- I express exactly how I *feel*.
- I pause to let it sink in.
- I hug my children and
- I tell them I love them.

- I reprimand poor behavior.
- I tell my children what they *did* wrong.
- I express exactly how I *feel*.
- I pause to let it sink in.
- I touch my children.
- I remind them that they are better than that; *they* are good; their *behavior* was bad.
- I hug my children and remind them how much I love them.
- When it's over, it's over!

PROCEED WITH SUCCESS

RETURN TO START

MANY years later, the once young father looked back on the time when he had first heard of the principles of One Minute Parenting. He was glad he had written down some of what he had learned from the original One Minute Father.

He'd put his notes into a little book and had given copies to people who inquired.

The man had remembered the friend who had referred him to The Father in the first place and had asked him if he wanted a copy as well.

The friend telephoned him later to say, "I can't thank you enough. I am *using* the three secrets of One Minute Parenting now myself. And it's already made a big improvement in *my* family!"

The man was pleased that other fathers were using One Minute Parenting. And he was glad he had given the text to others.

All those who had a copy of their own could read and reread it at their own pace until they could understand it and put it to good use themselves.

The Father knew full well the very practical advantage of repetition in learning anything new.

Before long, many others in the neighborhood had become One Minute Parents. Some of the parents had even given it to their older children to read.

And they, in turn, had done the same for others.

The neighborhood soon became a more enjoyable place to live.

One afternoon, as he sat in his home, the new One Minute Father knew he was fortunate.

He had given himself the gift of getting greater results in less time. He had time to think—to give his family the kind of help it needed.

He had time to exercise and stay healthy.

He did not experience the emotional and physical stress other fathers experienced.

He knew that because he felt less stress in his life, he would live longer and better.

And he knew that many of the other people who used One Minute Parenting in their homes were enjoying the same benefits.

Both his children had learned to like themselves and to want to behave themselves. They had not had to face problems that many other families knew. But his family had done more than avoid the common pains of frustration and failure. They experienced a rare pleasure. They knew the comfort of a happy home.

Then the new One Minute Father got up from his favorite chair and walked around his den.

He was deep in thought.

He felt good about himself—as a person and as a father. His caring about his family had paid off handsomely. He had the love and affection of every member of his family.

He knew he had become a very effective father because his children had learned to like themselves and to want to behave themselves.

And perhaps most important of all, he enjoyed *him*self.

SUDDENLY the man heard his wife's voice. "Sorry to interrupt you, honey. But there is a young woman on the telephone. She wants to come and talk to us about the way we parent."

The young mother, who had watched her husband communicate with her children and had seen how much things had improved in her family, had also begun to use the same method. She offered, "I'd be happy to join you for the discussion if you'd like."

The man said, "Would you, honey? That would be great. Maybe we could tell her what we've learned about how a mother and a father use the same system differently to get the same results."

The new One Minute Father was pleased. He knew that more mothers and fathers were taking a greater interest in their children. Some of them were as keen as he had been to learn how they might do a better job of raising their children.

The Father's family was active and happy. They enjoyed one another. And so did those who knew them. It felt good to be in his position.

"Come any time," he told the caller.

And soon he and his wife found themselves talking with a bright young woman. "We're glad to share our parenting secrets with you," the new One Minute Father said.

"I will only make one request of you."

"What is that?" the visitor asked.

"Simply," the parent began, "that you . . .

*

Share It With Others

*

the
end

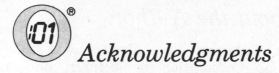 *Acknowledgments*

Over the years I have learned a great deal from many individuals. I would like to acknowledge and give a public praising to the following people:

A Special Praising to:
Dr. Gerald Nelson, the originator of the One Minute Scolding, for what he taught me about separating behavior and personal worth.
And to:
Dr. Kenneth Blanchard for what he taught me about personal humor and prosperity.
Dr. Dorothy Briggs, for what she taught me about a child's self-esteem.
Superintendent Midge Carroll for what she taught me about violated children and violent criminals.
Dr. Thomas Connellan for what he taught me about demonstrating positive reinforcement.
Dr. Charles McCormick for what he taught me about touching.
Dr. Kenneth Majer for what he taught me about goal setting.
Earl Nightingale for what he taught me about the Greatest Secret in the World.
Dr. Carl Rogers for what he taught me about personal honesty and openness.
Nelson Burton, Sr., and *Nelson Burton, Jr.,* for what they taught me about winning.

About the Author

Dr. Spencer Johnson is chairman of Candle Communications Corporation, a lecturer, and a communications consultant who helps people experience less stress and more success in their lives through better communication.

In 1977, long before he co-authored the best-selling book *The One Minute Manager* (with Kenneth Blanchard, Ph.D.), Dr. Johnson was using his now famous three-step method in his own home to teach his children how to like themselves and want to behave themselves.

He spent the next few years listening to other parents who were learning how to use his method with the same success. Many of their practical suggestions are in this book.

Dr. Johnson is also the widely acclaimed author of more than a dozen books dealing with medicine and psychology, including the popular *ValueTale* series of children's books. More than four million copies of his books are now in use.

Dr. Johnson's education includes a degree in psychology from the University of Southern California, an M.D. degree from the Royal College of Surgeons in Ireland, and medical clerkships at Harvard Medical School, Los Angeles Children's Hospital, and the Mayo Clinic.

He has also served as consultant for the Center for the Study of the Person, Human Dimensions in Medicine Program, and for the Office of Continuing Education at the School of Medicine, University of California in La Jolla.

Dr. Johnson is currently writing two new books.